Central Review

Vol. 20

Cover Image: "for when you feel alone" Shy Barteck

Cover Design: Lauren Cole

Central Review would like to thank
Professor Jeffrey Bean for all his
guidance as our advisor, and
Professor Matthew Roberson, without
whom the magazine would not be in print.

Central Review thrives thanks to the generosity of
our supporters. We are especially grateful to
Sandra Seaton, whose
contribution to this issue reminds us that creative
work matters—
and deserves champions.

Want to become a part of our story? Reach out
about donating or supporting our next issue.

Contents

Letters from the Editors

Dear Readers,

Thank you once again for meeting me in the pages of *Central Review*'s latest edition. If this is your first time being here, welcome. We are so glad to have you.

To everyone who submitted, thank you. Brenna and I would be lost at sea were it not for the bravery of so many artists willing to be vulnerable and share their work with us. If you were not featured in this Spring's publication, please know that the exclusion of your work is in every way a consequence of limited resources, and in no way a reflection of the merit or quality of what you have to say. Please never stop having something to say.

Each new issue of *Central Review* becomes my favorite, and Volume 20 is no exception; there is much to admire about this collection. For one, it is alive with visual art of all flavors. A sincere thank you to Shy Barteck for her photo "for when you feel alone", which we have chosen to feature as V20's cover. Thanks are due as well to Lauren Cole, the savvy designer behind the cover as a whole.

I also want to thank the staff of *Central Review*, whose quick application of taste is what pulls the statue from the marble and gives us our magazine.

I hope that *Central Review: Volume 20* ferries you, reader, fully into the thaw, where you float through the pines.

I will see you there.

Yours, very truly,
Liv O'Toole

Dear reader,

Welcome to Volume 20 of *The Central Review*. I use the word welcome with great intention. Colleges across the country, including our own, have faced challenges and pressures this semester that impact our entire university community.

But *Central Review* has always been about collaboration. The staff, the contributors, the genres—a great many people are involved in crafting each edition of this magazine, and the result offers readers a glimpse into the art being created here at CMU.

Liv and I are so grateful to everyone who submitted to *Central Review* this semester. Thank you for sharing a piece of yourselves with us and trusting us to publish it.

Thank you also to our wonderful and encouraging advisor, Jeffrey Bean, and to Matthew Roberson, who for the past two semesters has helped bring *Central Review* back into print.

Thank you, Shy Barteck, for gracing our cover with your photography, and Lauren Cole, for designing the cover.

Finally, thank you once more to Lauren Cole, as well

as Bri Edgar, for creating some of the best social media content around.

To the staff and my fellow Editor-in-Chief, Liv, I love you all!

I am so proud of *Central Review: Volume 20*. I hope, dear reader, that as you explore this collection you are not only filled with that same pride, but with a feeling of belonging too.

You *belong* here, so stay in these pages as long as you'd like. There's a lot to love, and a lot of comfort to be found. Thank you for reading.

All my love,
Brenna Dean

For Our Nerves

By Aldo García-Pájaro

I've lost interest in conversation
Beneath the waves of Malibu
It's the saddest confirmation
That I need somebody new

Since our years of frustration
You haven't aged a day
What a Twisted complication
You're far stuck in your ways

There's an itch gone unscratched
From the sand in my shorts
Wood set ablaze, gone is the match
We down Whitney for our nerves

Just because Mike told you to
Doesn't mean you must
Huron tides crash and I miss you
The one I once could trust

Floyd

By Morgan Hughley

Kinky hair
obsidian skin

always matched with
colored shirts
and silver bracelets

the ruthless acts against us is tasteless
you say freedom's on the tip of my tongue
well i can't taste it
face it

they never wanted us to excel
from bondage to officers
they don't think we can tell

or comprehend their strategies
And fathom injustice in our society

but from what I can see
we're all well aware

unfortunately
gods not the only man i fear

i want my reparations
i don't wanna be scared

give it time they say
the only time they be givin' is behind a cell
then they always wonder why we rebel

i'm a young black woman
I was born to excel.

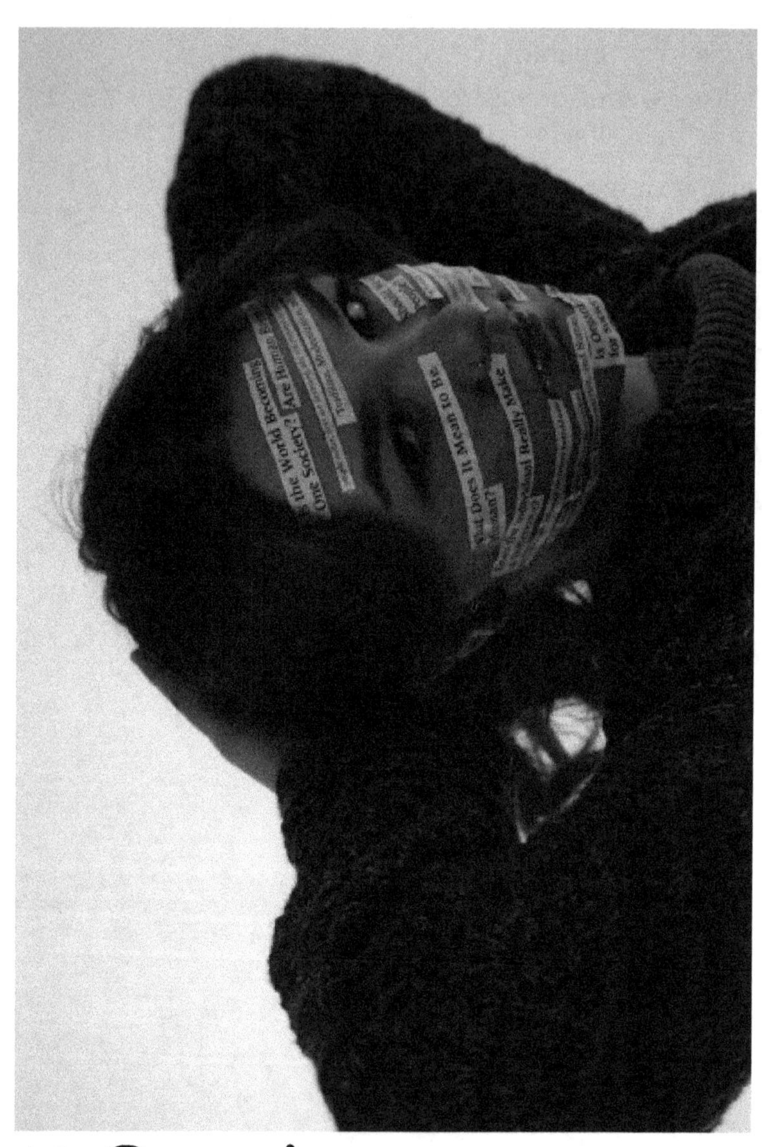

10 Questions

By Chandler Fox

When I Die

By Ella Hunnewell

When I die
Let me rot.
Don't violate me with chemicals,
Don't exchange my blood for formaldehyde,
Put me under the willow tree
And let me nourish the world.
Let me feel the breeze and dance again.
Let me harbor the small, fragile creatures.
Let me bloom each spring and
Let the snow blanket me each winter.
When I die
Let me root
Into the earth.
Let the worms feast
As my cares soak into the soil
And my fears drain with it.
Let me grow taller and stronger
Than I could ever be in this life
Or the last life.
When I die
Let me be beautiful.
When I die
Let me be.

Funeral Conversations

By Madison Schamber

Hey, how are you?
How have things been?
This small-talk is boring me
to death,

seeing family that I haven't seen
probably since last Thanksgiving,
or maybe the year before,

we've come together once more
to honor the deceased, and
spend quality time with family and friends.

Relatives which we see only once a year,
for formality's sake, because it's tradition.

Are you Kara? Or Katie?
Which aunt or uncle is your parent?
It doesn't really matter anyway.
I'll pretend to place a name to a face

Familiar strangers approach me.
Look how much you've grown!
I haven't seen you since you were
only two years old.

How's your daughter?

The last time I saw my niece
she was still wearing diapers,
now she's forming sentences.

Oh, you have another kid?
Anyway,

I'm sorry for your loss,
I offer my condolences.
I wish I had more to say, but I suppose
I'll see you at the next funeral.

I am a Cento

By Elizabeth Holloway

I am a made-up dinosaur & a real dinosaur & who knows maybe
Still in the non-genius condition of wanting.
"She is an insatiable nymphomaniac," but they don't
Feed small and necessary creatures.
A good dinosaur but also sort of evil & sometimes loving no one.

Beelzebub. Brachiosaur. Bubble-headed. I don't know how I stay alive.
Warm another pot of coffee, while the dishes pile up in the sink.
Somewhere inside the delicate center of my chest, a string,
A butterfly sanctuary where I would read.
Selfish bitch. I wish I could fry and eat them.

I like the lady horses best. It's metaphysical when girls
Wear pink but write poems & love what can die,
A fly or a mosquito, a cricket or a bee, the Luna moth.
It's a Darwinian thing, I know, but real tears, hard love,
They are hard to read. We learn to read.

The universe does not revolve around the human being
We are the gods who can unmake
A made-up dinosaur & a real dinosaur.
I'm not ready, maybe I am not yet tired enough.
Don't look back, Dinosaur. Dust is dust.

[Chen Chen, Mark Halliday, Vicki Hudspith, Ross Gay,
Sarah Manguso, Jason Shinder, Ada Limón, Jamaal May,
Fatima Asghar, Lauren Espada, Yusef Komunyakaa, Mathew
Olzmann, Tiana Clark, Steve Tomasko, Lisel Mueller, Jessica
Goodheart]

Summers in Franklin, Kentucky

By Brittany Hanner

We run barefoot through the rolling
hills of Kentucky fields at sunset.
Dusk animates the wilderness, brings
life scuttling from burrows and hiding
places between deep red maples and mighty
oaks. The cicadas call out to us as we search
for their abandoned shells amongst the brown
bark they cling to. Down at the bottom
of the steep slope next to Granny's house,
a river runs deep through the divide.
A shallow Mariana, trenched so far down
we cannot see it from the top of the hill.
I used to think if it were to rain too heavily
Granny's house would slide down
and drift away to wherever the river runs.
Granny would be sitting on the paint-peeled
porch swing curled up with a handstitched quilt.
She would join Paw once more, hand in hand
on that rusted swing, until we see them again.

In Spite of the Odds

By Cailey Calhoun

the rate at which the universe
began expanding was in the infinitesimal
interval between being too slow
-leading to complete collapse of all mass
as atoms shrunk into themselves-
and being too fast
- which would spread light and darkness
into far away corners of nothingness
where they couldn't comfort each other-

but in spite of the odds, we're here
there's trash to be taken out
laundry to fold, there's tears and arguments
about who left the door unlocked
there's mold in the coffee mugs,
but only because i might have left them
in the car

there's movies we can't watch,
places we can't visit
there's seafood we throw up
and fruits we're allergic to

there's stray hairs,
frayed ends,
       broken nails,
stubbed toes,

broken bones,
          spotty service,
cold showers,
itchy sweaters,
          stuffy rooms and noses,

there's nights with music that's way too loud
and nightmares at five a.m. leaving us
too scared to go back to sleep
there's so much that can go wrong
while we're here. we're here.

The Pines

By Lillian Scarborough

"Don't bother the earth spirit who lives here. She is working on a story. It is the oldest story in the world and it is delicate, changing." – Joy Harjo

The pines speak with ease on days like today,
when you crave kinships embrace-
Mother Nature–She never forgot your name.

The river winds, whispering their echoing melody-
She hums their names in the roots embrace,
The pines speak to appease on days like today.

Each pine has its rings, each ring a child's burning flame,
escaping the cruel boarding school they once faced.
Mother Nature–She still speaks your name.

When I hug these pines, I'm held in countless ways,
Their damp eyes within the evergreen laced.
The pines speak to release on days like today.

Spirits and stories nourish this land, pine needles aim
them to constellations at nights embrace.
Mother Nature–She writes your name.

Fathers of the forest, whispering wisdom, sweet and tame:
"omiimi-ziibing mikwendang gaye giiwedin-anang"
As they sway, the pines speak with ease on days like today-
She never forgot your name.

"omiimi-ziibing mikwendang gaye giiwedin-anang" is
Anishinaabemowin for *"a river that remembers, and a star that can lead one home."*

A Symphony of Green
By Kaelynn Blake

First line by Robert Fanning

So begins the song of the earth
A gentle tuning hum of wind
The light tapping of branches
      a conductors wand
And the crashing symbols of a canopy of leaves
A symphony of green

The crickets join the chorus
      a string section
And the croaking frogs become bassdrums
Birds
      The woodwinds
Whistle tangled overlapping melodies
The earth itself
      The brass
A silent countermelody of movements.

Stop with me and listen
Let the sound become you
      Audience of one.

A CONSIDERATION OF ORGANIZED SPORTS AND RELIGION

By Rowan Schachermeyer

Short sports often bore, and can classify
As a massive waste of time, simply a
Desire to end and begin with a slither, a pop
Of color, white and whirly, topsy turvy,
Around and around, once more, once more.

Jesus kickflips,
And then he falls and
We just seem to watch as he
Falls and falls, liberated
By the small and sweet knowledge that it
Isn't just us.

It soars past, old leather ball
Rough and cracking,
Passed from hand to hand.
Father to son,
Bright lights and bigger dreams,
Forced down upon a
Soul created for one purpose,
To carry on.

Duality Pt. II: Masking

By Almir Martin

Heavenly Bodies

By Dominic Tatrai

<u>Mercury</u>
Mercury saw them beyond the Oort Cloud, so deep in each other's arms it was difficult to distinguish the two. Scandalous to be sure, but the whole affair excited something deep within Mercury's core, so he kept it secret. In a way he became the third participant, a guardian of their love, enjoying the cool of their shadow.

<u>Venus</u>
Venus found the whole thing offensive. Perhaps if it was done honestly, out in the open, under the purity of starlight, then maybe Venus could be swayed. Yet they scurried around like displeasing little asteroids, crashing into each other in the most vulgar of tones. Venus kept the obscenity quiet, however; it would hurt Jupiter the most, and Venus understood that, with a small sampling of patience, the perfect opportunity would arise for Venus to reveal the whole farce. Jupiter would be broken. Venus would feel whole.

<u>Earth</u>
Earth understood how wrong it was, but that only made it much more exciting. It started innocently enough, small nods of acknowledgment, carefree hangouts without tension, yet Earth knew, even then, that she was falling into his orbit. The day would come for their love to be exposed, eclipsing any good will

Earth had formed with the solar system. But until that day of annihilation, she would keep in his trajectory, let him heat her simmering core.

Mars
Mars left them to their little dalliances. Who cares who was hooking up with who? There were others to worry about, like Phobos and Deimos. Deimos would be his soon, that much was certain. Collision, followed by unification. But Phobos was escaping his pull. That simply would not do. Mars would have what is rightfully his.

Jupiter
As much as it pained him, Jupiter would leave the two be, leave them to their little affair. Jupiter was a lover, that much he knew. If Jupiter could, he would hold everyone in his orbit, safe and within reach. However, Jupiter understood the importance of space. Venus still held a grudge, made clear by her passing glances, each one holding a story of resentment and pain. Suffocating, she called him. All consuming. Like a black hole. That's what she called his love: a black hole. It was a lie, of course. If his love was a black hole, she never would have escaped.

Saturn
It annoyed the ever loving shit out of Saturn that Earth was getting some and she was getting bupkis. Neptune was pulling away again, not accepting her love for what it is. Maybe she was jealous; who wouldn't be? Saturn had the best rings around. But wouldn't that make Neptune want her even more? The whole thing made Saturn just want to shriek into the void.

Uranus

Uranus had other things to worry about, like being the butt of everyone's jokes.

Neptune

Neptune wanted out, out of it all. They were all caught in each other's grasp, caught in the tug and pull of it. If only they could break free, they would be set to follow their own hearts. She had to get away from Saturn. If it were up to Saturn, they would merge their elements into one, one body made from the carcass of two.

Pluto

Pluto hated the lot of them. He was caught in the same orbit as them, wasn't he? Influenced by the same dreamy song of gravity? Yet here Pluto was, cast away, deprived of rightful status. Not a planet, they said. Technicality, they said. Pluto could read between the lines. He's fluent in fake smiles and false niceties. But he was content, nonetheless; soon the ties that bound them would be broken. Earth was mere clay in his hands. One mention of their affair, and the whole solar system would come undone. Then they would understand that Pluto held the same grace as any other.

Sun

The Sun was happy. They were the biggest star in the sky, after all. Everyone was in their pull, living their lives, unaware of the true nature of things. They could fight it all they want. The Sun played on a different time scale; just yesterday they were formed, and it will only take another day before the Sun expands and takes what's theirs, enjoying the sweet taste of heavenly bodies.

The Story of an Elderly Man Who Didn't Tell It

By Tarry Palmer

After "A Story" by Li-Young Lee

Sad is the man who is asked for a story
And can't come up with one.
his mind once sharp with detail,
now a nebulous puzzle where the
pieces don't seem to fit.
A blank stare from ashen eyes
narrates what his tale has become.

Knuckles swollen like knots on a birch tree.
Bones as brittle as the stale bread
he feeds the pigeons on Sunday afternoons
in Central Park. Playing chess with strangers
wearing a dark grey sweater with holes in the elbows
from leaning on the red and cream-colored brick.

Saturated socks stuck to his feet from puddles he trudged
through with the worn soles of his sneakers
on his way to see his wife at the cemetery.
His name in marble with no death date
leers back at him. Purple lilies wrapped in
tissue paper, a token of a love that conquered death.

A Sunset on Scram Lake

By Carter Moleski

Flames die and candles cry.
Wax tears drip down their faces
as the stars climb the sky
outside the kitchen window.

The lake begins to glow with moonlit fire.
Pulsing purple smoke sneaks into the sky
as the neon orange sun dives into the deep
blue, slowly sinking
into a sanctuary of sunfish and silence.

Paddle boards and boats driven
by the neighbors' grandchildren drift
back to the docks, letting the dance of waves
come to a calm conclusion.

So when the final porch light closes its eyes,
and the only sounds that remain come from
the whispers on Mom and Dad's TV,
let it be known that even the dreams
painted by turtles portray the stunning
sunsets on Scram Lake.

An Ode to My Broken Microwave

By Gabrielle Steele

My Jupiter in the kitchen,
how my mediocre meals orbited inside
your trepid storm. You are shattered in a ludicrous mess
on my linoleum floor. I miss your beeps, causing
a discombobulated xylophone-sounding hole
in my heart. Bamboozled, I wail for you.

A single earthquake in Mississippi
fixed our fate. Your rigid metal frame lay
dormant. No embalming could restore
your postmortem body. My dinners stay frozen
as if they were a lover longing for your radiation.
I ask once more, how could you fall off the counter?

How could you abandon me
and your Chinese takeaway brethren?
The leftovers curdle, mold, and revolt against
your selfish malfunction, leaving them to decay.
Oh, why would you leap to these dusty depths
when your warmth fed my starving stomach?

Floating

By Janessa Shepard

Off the Coast of Beaver Island

The stars send glowing warmth despite the cold
as gentle waves undo my years of pain.
This lake, this void, releases memories old.

Water laps my skin, searching for a hold,
while minnows flee what cannot be contained.
The stars send glowing warmth despite the cold.

Orion, Aries, Cancer knows. Behold
my secrets, World. Please, let them entertain.
This lake, this void, releases memories old.

The moon is silent, hearing what has been told
as he observes—though he has nothing to gain.
The stars send glowing warmth despite the cold.

Above, the comets race to jeer and scold,
their flash of light a sign that speaks in vain.
This lake, this void, releases memories old.

I whisper truths to lights of green and gold—
they dance above and ask to hear again.
The stars send glowing warmth despite the cold
as this lake, this void, releases memories old.

Cemetery Angels

By Autumn Malinowski

You crawl to the cemetery angels to plead
your best angle, but this funereal light looks unforgiving
on everyone. You've accepted mortality
the second you stepped foot in the outback
graveyard, an attempt to bypass the church confessional,
voiceless in fear of your last words escaping. Unkept
defining confessions, written in moss, lay in willow tree
alcoves and grief-trodden grass, you can't help but wonder
who will write yours. Sentinel marble stares guard over
the stillness, preserving the crux of where the living forget
and the rest forcibly move on. Each pass of wind feels
like a dying breath as you collapse into a defeated kneel in
        the dirt,
giving way to the weight of all your hurt, you believe
        your fate
to be ghostwritten as you die at your own hand.
        Suffocating under the Earth's
eternal embrace.

# for when you feel alone 1

By Shy Barteck

Still

By Kayla Thatcher

Your clothes are still in the wash. I need to put mine in.
The waves still crash, but their noise isn't soothing
      like it was in North Carolina.
Scissors never cut paper. Rocks don't break scissors.
      Paper doesn't cover rock.
Midnight McDonald's runs are silent, a voiceless
      drive into town.
You still owe me $36.73 from our dinner at Applebee's.
      I'll add it to your no-more-growing tab.
My screen time has gone down. So have my notifications.
Instagram messages are silent, no response to be expected.
Our list of movies is frozen in time, growing cobwebs
      over the years.
I have more money now. No more impulsive purchases
      with rolling eyes and quiet laughter as your elbow
      digs into my arm.
I haven't turned his post notifications off, even though
      we can't enjoy it together.
My notes app grows silent, the *Awesome Quotes* folder
      suspended where it is.
You still have my sweatshirt tucked between two others
      in your closet. I don't want to get it back.
I'll never stop sending "I love you". Not even when your
      number is given away.

Estrogenized Sestina

By June Maslowski

I am a girl—no, I am a woman
now. I am the ants. Many
tiny sugar-bound fighters.
I am peaches now. I am bruised
and soft. When they bring me
back, there will be nothing left.

I am forgotten, lost—left
alone in my room now, a woman
told not to eat, not yet. I am me,
that, I am sure. I am them, many.
I hear their pained cries, the bruised
throwing fist after fist, unfair fighters.

I am armed to the teeth—a fighter
knows that a fang left
at home could get you bruised,
could get you killed. I am the woman
you saw dance, I am the many
women you saw dance, she is me.

I am a dog—I am feral, dangerous. Me
and my girls will fuck you up, we are fighters,
snaggle-toothed stragglers. We have seen many
a brawl, and this shit ain't no scare. Go left
and you can't miss us, a pack of women,
beautiful, brave, bruised.

I am a realist—you can't do work without bruising.
Can't keep your hair if you keep lying to me.
Can't be a woman, just can't be a woman.
Can't give in when I have always been a fighter.
Can't bring back a person that left.
Can't be pretend when there are this many.

I am a human—if you look you'll find many
of us. In your diners, we sit at the bar, bruised,
but smiling, the times are tough, but joy hasn't left.
Maybe someday we'll talk, you'll sit next to me
and we'll have a chat about the fighter
that I was (and in many ways, still am), and the woman.

But until then this woman will sit with her many friends,
sharing tales of fights and ogling bruises on shoulders.
If you ever want to chat with me, we're right here. We never left.

Sullivan

By Courtney Hanses

The snow had come early that year. Too early. The trees were still covered in leaves. The animals were yet to hibernate. None of that could stop the blanket of white that fell from the sky.

New York City was constantly bustling with millions of people every day. It wasn't just a home; it was a whole world compressed into 300 square miles. Some would spend their entire lives in the bubble and never exhaust from it.

Arthur Sullivan watched this world go by from the window of his hospital room. He'd gone in for a persistent pain in his chest and quickly learned that his time on this Earth was limited. He was a mere thirty-six years old. His hair was golden and yet to grey. The wrinkles on his face were just beginning to form. He was far too young to be dying.

He'd never wedded, and had no children either. His estranged younger brother was his only family left and all he'll ever have.

October 7, 1956
Dear Brother,

I'm a dying man. Cancer, late stage. They say I have a few weeks, maybe a month.

My looming demise has left me pondering and reflecting on my life and everyone in it. I think about Mother, and how she spent her every day doing her best to give us a good life. I reminisce about Father, and his bravery that inspired me to follow in his footsteps. And I wonder about you, James. My kid brother.

> *What are you up to these days? Are you and Anne doing well? Do you have any children? What about your career? You were always so bright growing up. I hope that has paid off for you.*
>
> *What's Pennsylvania like? Is it much different than New York? I still fail to see why you left and went so far away. At the same time, I entirely understand. However, would you be able to come visit me this month? There's some places in the city I'd like to visit one last time.*
>
> *Please take this as my dying wish.*

I hope to hear from you soon,
Arthur Sullivan

Arthur hadn't seen his brother in over a decade. Their only contact was the occasional letter and yearly birthday cards. He returned from the war eleven years ago to an empty home with nothing but a note on the counter.

Mother passed last spring. I can't stay here anymore. My new address is 114 N Oak, Harrisburg, PA 17110. I'm moving there with my wife, Anne.
James

Arthur was unable to forget the gutted feeling that pulsed through him upon finding James' letter. That feeling struck him each time he unfolded and reread his brother's letter whenever he wanted to reach him.

He'd won the war, though. Promoted to captain in the Navy. Father must've been looking down at him so proudly now. He had to be. Arthur was the perfect son. His father's legacy was going to be remembered for ages.

Thomas Sullivan, Commander in Chief of the United States Navy, 1916-1924. And his son, Arthur Sullivan, Navy Captain, 1944-1950.

When he was feeling lonely or down, Arthur recited those lines to himself to feel closer to his father. They were all a lie, though. Commander Thomas Sullivan never met Captain Arthur Sullivan. Thomas may have known Arthur, but he did not know the Captain. Arthur was always aware of this, whether he was ready to accept it or not.

A week passed. Arthur's physical condition only worsened. He could feel the hourglass of his life draining to the bottom.

He rarely received any mail. When he did, it was always something such as bills or reminders about something. All he could do was to wait anxiously to hear back from his brother. On October 17th, James' reply had made its way to him.

October 12, 1956
Arthur,

I received your letter. It's unfortunate to hear that you'll be leaving us so soon. Thirty-something is awfully young to die these days, don't you think? Part of me has been waiting for an excuse to return to New York. I guess this one counts. I can be there on October 20th. Don't die quite yet and be ready for my arrival.

James

October eighth, ninth, tenth, eleventh, twelfth, thirteenth, fourteenth, fifteenth, sixteenth, seventeenth, eighteenth, nineteenth. Arthur X-ed off each day on his calendar as they passed him. Life was nothing but a waiting game and some time to plan everywhere he'd like to go in order of significance, in the event he didn't survive the whole journey. A morbid thought, but one he had to consider.

Arthur had fuzzy but fond memories of his childhood home. That's where his family was still together. Mom and Dad would tuck him into bed in that house. Everywhere else he lived afterwards failed to feel as warm.

There was a certain tree in Central Park that young Arthur and his father raced to and played catch under. Saturdays weren't the same without that tree. Arthur hadn't gone back to that area of the park in years from a fear of it not being how he remembered it to be all those years ago.

Arthur's elementary-school years were an easy time in his life full of carefree and naive bliss. He wasn't old enough yet to comprehend why Father wasn't home anymore. He still had dreams and a love for baseball and drawing.

As much as it pained him, he had to face his mother's grave. The past decade had filled him with too much guilt and remorse to visit her. He hated himself for being overseas as his mom faded away before he even knew anything was wrong.

...

James arrived in the city early that Saturday. He felt sick at the thought of seeing his older brother as weak as he saw his mom a decade ago. So much had happened in all those years. He moved states, got a job in something he really cared about, and had a child of his own. His life could not have been more different than it was the last time he and Arthur saw each other. James was content and fulfilled with how things were turning out for him. So, when he received his brother's letter, it felt like a bullet from his past life struck him right in the chest.

He looked back at the envelope he received from Arthur a few short weeks ago. Room 104 was what housed his wilting brother. He gave the door two gentle knocks and waited for a response.

A weak and strained voice replied with a "Hello? Come in," seconds after.

James pushed the door open and felt his face run cold upon seeing the state Arthur was in. He was thin and pale. The fullness of his face was all gone. The forms of his ribs were poking through the fabric of his shirt. His eyes were bloodshot and lightless. James understood immediately that his brother had little time left. "Arthur?"

"James! Thank you for coming, truly."

"Shall we begin our journey?" James fought the urge to cry. He wanted to stay strong for his brother's sake. He watched Arthur struggle to sit up and get out of his bed. "Can you walk?"

"Hardly. I have a chair over there that you could push me in," he replied and pointed to the corner of the room. Even things as simple as short sentences were hard for him to get out without coughing or having to catch his breath afterwards.

The brothers set off on their trip through memory lane. The October snow still blanketed the city. James couldn't remember the last time he saw it like this so early in the season.

790 W. Jefferson looked much different than it had twenty years ago. The siding was blue instead of cream. The tree in the front lawn now towered over the house. There were children playing with snow on the front lawn.

Arthur was a little kid again. Bright-eyed and full of hope. His naive dreams about pleasing his father flooded his mind and commanded his emotions. That was the yard he stood in when he waved goodbye to his mother and went off to begin his military training. That was the house he was in when he held a baseball for the last time. That was where his dreams were still alive. "Thank you for bringing me here," was all he could get out. His feelings were overflowing and had to be contained.

Central Park was a lot busier than Arthur remembered. He pointed James towards where he and his father's tree stood. Arthur could envision the first day he beat his dad in a race towards it. But now, the tree was grey and bare. His tree was dead. He spent so long avoiding it, and now it's nothing but a husk. It was a horrifying sight and a reminder that Arthur's joyful childhood was gone and buried in time.

Eastwood Elementary was the same way. A shallow corpse of what Arthur remembered it to be. It had closed down and been repurposed for some generic office building.

...

It was evening when the brothers arrived at Cedar Cemetery. James had buried their mother by himself. He never quite processed the grief and left town soon after. He headed towards her grave. It was dirty and overgrown. "You never came and visited her, did you?"

Arthur's heart stopped for a moment. He gave a sorrowful "No. I couldn't."

"What do you mean you couldn't? You've been so close to her all these years." James snapped back. He intended on being patient and civil this weekend but the pain he felt for his mother was too overwhelming.

His brother's fate was not going to make James keep his grievances contained.

"The guilt, it was too much. I'm sorry. I feel better now, though. This was the closure I've needed." Arthur, too, had yet to process the grief felt about his mother. But seeing her name etched into a stone had made it all become real in his mind. He felt soft tears roll down his cheek.

"James?"

"Yes?"

"Can we visit one more thing? I think it'll be the last thing I need closure about. Father's grave. Can we find it? He has to be here, right?"

James and Arthur went down aisle after aisle until they spotted their last name on a stone. They were cold and exhausted and so sure it had to be him.

The two stared at the grave. The small, tattered American flag in front of it swayed in the wind. A shower of silence fell over the cemetery. James has had a lot of thoughts about his brother's obsession with their father over the years. "Why do you care so much, anyway?"

"Why don't you care at all?" Arthur snapped back. A festering grudge built upon years of misunderstanding forced its way out.

"I don't have memories with him like you do. I don't have a special tree or a book he'd read to me. He's just a man to me. I've got no desire to 'make him proud.' I live my life the way I want to."

Arthur felt the sharpness of his brother's words hit him all over. "Well, how else was I supposed to connect with him? You and mother never did anything. I couldn't simply move on and act like he never existed, okay?"

Throughout his time as a soldier, Arthur

couldn't care less about the nation or the war or the conflicts of the world. He didn't enlist because of passion or patriotism. He did it because he couldn't escape the portrait with his father's looming gaze watching him in his home. If Arthur didn't continue his legacy, who would? So, he put away his passions and the goals he would've pursued had Father lived longer.

There was some regret about that, of course. If Arthur had known that his life was going to be cut so short, would he have chosen a different path? He concluded that he wouldn't have been able to. His desire to connect with Father was too strong to let himself settle down into a simple life. He was too blinded by this dream to see the tragedy of it all.

What would Arthur Sullivan's legacy be? A soldier in his father's footsteps? The boy who spent his whole life chasing after some sense of approval? A man who gave up everything he ever wanted to do in pursuit of an unachievable goal? Would he even have a legacy at all?

...

Arthur didn't sleep at all that night. He was too tired, too sick, too devastated at his own choices. At 4:46 AM, he looked out the window in the direction of the cemetery and painfully cried out "I've got nothing else so, did I make you proud, Father?"

On October 21st at 4:47 AM, Arthur Sullivan passed on in his hospital bed. He died as a soldier would, alone and cold and wondering about all of what his life could've been.

...

Upon learning about his brother's approaching fate, James had purchased a plot in the cemetery and a stone to accompany it. He left the rest to whoever buried him. To the right of *Commander in Chief of the U.S. Navy Thomas Sullivan, 1887-1924* was simply *Sullivan, 1919-1956.*

Moonlit Love

By Kayla Thatcher

I
Every night we would look at the stars
Shooting across like planes of war.
We'd sneak out late to search for Mars
Wishing on rocks for one week more.

Though now I sneak out unescorted.
Sitting on the fresh-cut lawn
Beside her headstone, I'm transported
To simpler times, when we'd stay out till dawn.

Mars shines bright and the big frogs croak.
Between burial plots, I grow tired
As I wait in vain for her to wake.
Her grave is still as I lay beside it.

I miss my love with her jaded eyes.
But I find her comfort in the starry skies.

II
My love comes by more often than not,
Her eyes are tired and dimming each day.
She settles down in her usual spot
And runs her fingers down my grave.

I'm reminded of my final weeks
When we'd lie together about my condition.

She'd wheel me down to see the creek
To free me from my sterile prison.

Tonight the nearby water babbles
As I take my place by her side
The pain I see is immeasurable
An agony that won't leave her behind.

Without a heart I shouldn't feel
But all I wish is for time to heal.

III
She next returns when the sun is high.
I watch her come to a sudden stop.
Her gaze on mine, I cannot deny,
Makes my stalled heart drop.

Our names coated in disbelief
Are the first breaths to escape us.
Another brutal victim of grief
Gone too soon, they discuss.

My love's death shook the town-
Heartbreak in the second degree.
Tears follow her six feet down
But now my love is finally free

A farewell of daffodils and a headstone
And bringing my love forever home.

A Moment in Time

By Brianna Edgar

Тарасова Вечеря. Cherry Garden.
By Masha Smahliuk

Homage to the memory of Taras Shevchenko

A nightingale whispers among the cherry trees,
when mom calls the family for dinner, and
рідний двір holds onto the passing peace.

I wash my face in Dnipro's salty breeze
and cottage cheese вареники sweet scent,
when the nightingale sings among the cherry trees.

Grandma passes some salt. Dad cuts a piece
of sourdough. Dusk crawls. Silver crescent
watches рідних hold onto this peace.

Through the sunflower fields,
плугатарі trudge home singing, when
the nightingale replies from the cherry trees.

Honey sinks in my cup of raspberry tea.
The first sip fills me with summer сонце.
Рідний двір holds onto the passing peace.

But February will come, tearing down these
Shevchenko's dreams. Yet in the end,
the nightingale will sing among the trees,
and рідний дім will trust the coming peace.

"Let's Get Together Soon"

By Hannah Stout

For Grace. I miss you every day.

Lame pinky swears of meeting up,
talking on the phone
or stopping by for a quick seven
hour chat turns into
an early morning text message of
Did you hear? She died. Suicide.
Her mother tried
to do the same a year ago,
but lived.
Now you're brought together
in a coffin sized church with warm
glass-stained windows.
Your lies sit in a back pew
paying their respects.
You vow that once the service
ends you'll constantly check
on your friends—for the next six months.
Then those common lies
will slither their way back
up, spreading awareness
as to why you can't hangout,
chat or meet up for a cup of coffee.
Family and friends' ugly cry
but you remain cold like the November
ground she is to be buried in because crying
shows you are broken too.
The pastor recites John 16:22
but you only look ahead.

Guilt tugs at your shirt
like a child begging for attention
as your friend sits in a compact
blue urn because a gunshot
to the head
took her final breath.
Grace was her name,
and gone is her soul.

I am five years old

By Kayla Thatcher

sitting on my bedroom floor
my dolls surrounding me.

I am seven years old
sitting on the basement floor
my bucket of dolls
open in the corner.

I am nine years old
with my best friend,
my Barbie Dreamhouse
in my closet, the dolls
scattered on the carpet.

I am eleven years old.
I open a ballerina Barbie
for Christmas.
My sister's boyfriend
is there. This is the first time
I am embarrassed of them.

I am thirteen years old.
My bin of dolls sits under my bed
untouched for most of the year.
I only get them out
when I'm alone.
But I think about their presence
constantly.

I am fifteen years old.
My dolls are long gone
probably donated
maybe thrown away.
I don't know.
I tell myself I don't care.
I find myself wishing
I had them again.

I am nineteen years old
sitting at the desk in my dorm,
two dolls lying in the drawers.
I pull them out late at night
to change their outfits
and brush their hair.
They're not the ones I knew,
But for just a moment
I am five years old once more.

'HATE TO LOVE YOU'

By Aparnaa Iyer

1. "I always preferred reading words on paper rather
than penning them down,
It wasn't something that held my fancy.
But when I met you and fell in love,
Putting phrases on sheets seemed easy.
But it was only after you pretended to love me and left
me broken,
That a poet was born and all the words in the universe
were left at my mercy."

2. "My eyes used to restlessly search for you,
Now I can't bear to even look at you.
I'm terrified of what I'll find written on your face,
Will there be any remnants of affection to trace?
There was a time when you did just about anything to
make me laugh,
But now your apathy can easily break my soul in half."

3. "I felt sure that you'd soon open your heart to me,
That my unconditional love would vanquish all hate.
But all you'd ever give me were these scraps,
Unbeknownst to this, I laid in wait,
But you turned a blind eye to my purity and kindness,
And sadly, so did Fate."

This House

By Aldo García-Pájaro

I look back on the house on the hill I used to speak of,
Nostalgia in stained glass I had not yet dreamed of
Curse these promised lands of concords and pomegranates,
Fruits so sweet we had taken them for granted
We procured this house to endure the hardest tempest
It lay under a darkest thundering sky just like the rest,
But it turns out lightning strikes twice, and it's messy
When a people forgive their vices and forget their blessings
So, I'll go into the forest and make the most of it
I'll pen letters to my closest friends and stay devoted
Rain will pour and ink will splatter, as may crimson things,
But no matter what this house won't shatter, I'll make
azure of it

Fantasizing with your Keys in my Pocket

By Aphelion Bates

I accidentally stole your building keys.
I wish that was some kind of metaphor, a joke
maybe, or a purposeful statement.
Imagine the intentionality of me demanding
a place in your life, a place in your home.
Imagine if you didn't have to let me inside.

I remember your door pin, I'd sneak right inside.
You didn't even notice that I had your keys,
I think it'd be easy to creep into your home
and make it ours. You might think I'm joking
but it's easy to make demands
when you're in this state. I meant

for this to be a statement
of love, and maybe somewhere inside
you know what led me to such demands.
You're so trusting, handing me your keys
and just forgetting like your safety's a joke.
Michigan will always be my home

but it's so cold and there's something homely
in your warmth. It's like an invitation, a statement,
leaving them in my pocket. I shouldn't joke
when your parents fear someone breaking inside.
Maybe they're paranoid for your keys
and the cold people like me, demanding

warmth you didn't offer, demanding
a way in when you're not home.
You're so overly cautious, except with your keys,
and I know what you dream of, regardless of statements
you make to soothe the good girl inside
you. Wanting to be kept can only be a joke

but independent girls don't make those jokes.
So I'll show I can be demanding,
I'd at least be a thorn in your side.
I won't just walk out of our home
without a fight, without a statement
to win you back, I won't give up your keys-

I'm not that brave though. I couldn't break into your home,
so leave with my heart, I'm just an idiot making a statement
I can't follow through on, because today I sent back your keys.

where the desert begins

By Megan Monroe

*(created using flower plaques around Central
Michigan University's campus)*

the air shimmers with the promise
of something wild—a *burning heart*
drifting on a *silver sage* breeze.

the forest will try to tempt you with a *blue
glow*, but the lake is a *false indigo*, a mirage
to pull you away from the *red satin* sand.

over the *prairie*, *dusk* will settle,
painting the skies with
a *brandywine sunset*.

the *canary*, *brilliant* in its song,
will flit the *blazing star* of its body
against the *rose mallow* clouds.

the last rays of the sun will catch
on the *matchsticks* and *firecrackers*,
a flickering *night light*

that dances off the grains of sand
in a *golden jubilee*, a makeshift *tango*
against the blue-black sky.

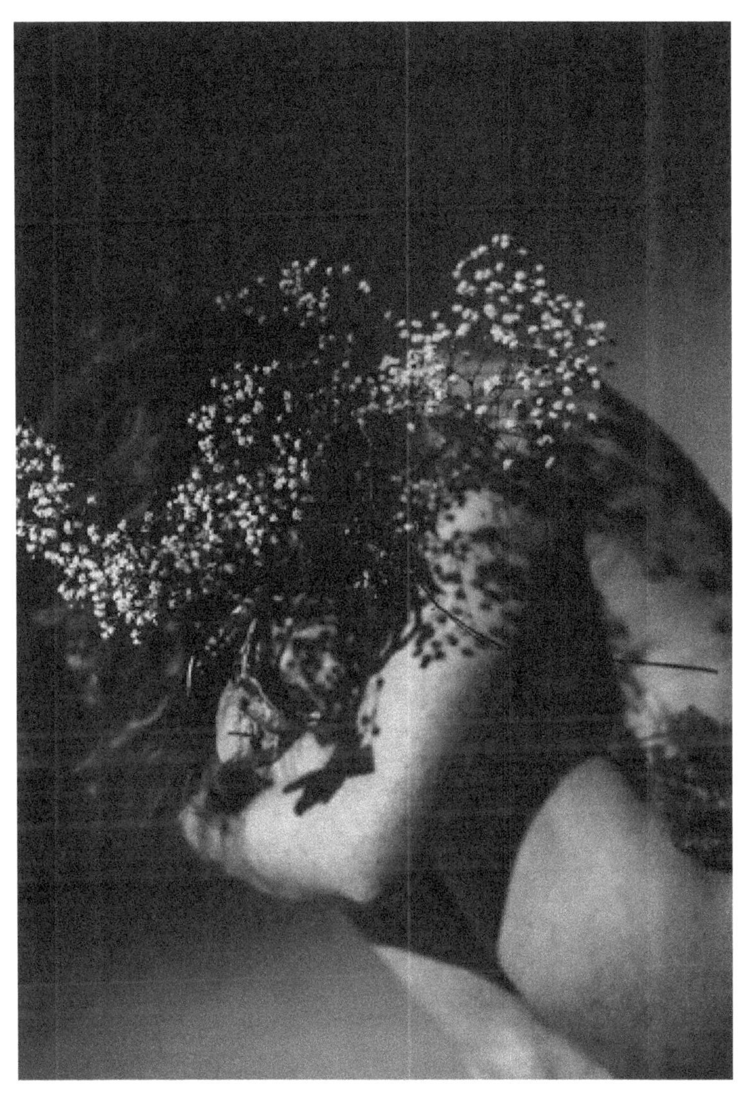

for when you feel alone 2

By Shy Barteck

wo-MEN

By Morgan Hughley

i find myself cradling

cradling myself to erase the pain of men with no boundaries,
men who impose their power with areas that are supposed
to be used to create something
beautiful but instead impose constant torment

constant torment to women with kind souls and joyful spirits
women who now endure sonder nights with pain,
lingering in places that were meant to create something
beautiful

lingering pain lingering disappointment in ourselves with
multiple could haves many should
haves and more would halves than needed

needed, thought, wanted you to understand no

no is not powerful as a female

no doesn't mean anything

don't we mean anything to this entitled species called male?

i thought this time was different
i thought you weren't "on that timing"

this time i'm the fool.

This time i'm stuck left with legs glued shut cradling

cradling myself to erase the pain of men with no boundaries,
men who impose their power with areas that are
supposed to be used to create something
beautiful but instead impose constant torment.

Ode to the Bat in the Wall

By Megan Miller

Midnight bane, that baroque bird
whose bearings exist as the balking of
of branched arms drubbing against
plaster barricades. Hoodlum bar none,
committing battery against bedroom brethren
whose faces bleed neurotic doldrums
that a bite-sized perforation in gable window
butterfly effects to morbid eventide skirmish
against nocturnal blight.

Phantom critter, that tintinnabulation of talons
on interior partitions. Heavy-metal rattle
of calcar locomotion, elastic extensions
ad lib against electric cords, chirp articulated
betwixt the tone of utilities. Equidistant rhythm
tapping tacit until twilight perforation
bites at eyes, venting varmint musicians release.

Sadist of trespass, sleep soured by airfoil
sides surfacing to scissor across ceilings. Shriek
of beast and man lacerates silence, savage
scrabble ensues. False vampire spots socket
and resigns to insulation, swaying secure
until moon's next scintillation while
resident personage becomes certified
convalescent psychotic listening to
chiropteran Mephistopheles for centuries.

love in the time of social atrophy

By Gwendolyn Kilpatrick

droplets (fine misting effervescent) encircle
me and you and the whirling winding
gray air while lovestruck passionate
eddies neatly jostle their subjects
(the leaves) in an imitative fashion of
me and you i suppose that's self-serving
hubris of mine (nature is as we are) and if
i told you that philosophically you would suppose
the same with a small laugh flinty
eyes and your hand harmonizing
my shoulder while we meander around asymmetric
potholes black skittering pebbles and
the asphalt wet from my melting heart

fantasy of a fantasy of a fantasy but in
real life you're animatedly talking next to
me of marquez and his classic
novel you never liked as cars approach us their
headlights illuminatory on your soft and my quaking
glow when you joke of the adoring funeralgoer (your
words a birdsong) and you pretend to feel
the character's earnestness (love temerity agony) and
say insightful things as i burst open next to
you in my mind with a tremulous cry that that's
me and your husband has died and i relish his
mossy headstone. but outside of my
mind i laugh and joke and try not to think of
me and you atrophizing apart as
it is and as it will be.

my eurydice

By Samantha Dave

i lost her twice—
my eurydice
with her hair that moved
like the roughest ocean
and the pale eyes of a ghost
that could see what wasn't there

i lost her in the shadow
of the trees that curled
and bent over the path
when the snap of a twig
ignited the fear sparked
by the vision of her lifeless eyes

hades' words rang through my head
for even he could not complete this task
as his hand rested on persephone's alabaster shoulder
as if she too might disappear

my eurydice
faded with the faintest gasp
into a cloud of mist
as beautiful as she
was the day she died
despite the fact that i begged
for her life—it's my fault she's gone

i wish it wasn't my fault
but i see her in a cloud of smoke
in the trees, the waves
every note i play sounds like her laugh
like the way she whispered *i love you*

my eurydice
i say three times into the mirror
as if that will bring her back

sweat poem

By June Maslowski

saltwater pearls spill
perilously, sent packing,
southbound patrolling.
slowly paddling slash
plummeting, smelly pilgrims sink.

panic signal, passion,
sodden palm. symphonies,
puny songs, primal, sliding.
partially sticky, perceptibly
sopping, perch skin.

persistent sultry pheromone,
sour pungency,
simply putrid, something
pretty. someone: "pee-yew!
shower, pigpen!"

sightly permeable shell, *per se*,
pooling, spilling past.
spiritually pleasing,
soft pleather soaked,
pampered, spoiled, panting.

steam preamble, singular penchant.
silly, pituitary shredded, perhaps.
sinful poetry student,

poor sap, painfully sexless,
praising sweat. please stop.

presenting, *self-portrait*:
signed, pit sniffer. pent-up?
sorta. perverted?
sure, probably. sometimes,
predilections stupefy.

person: "stupid poem stinks,
poet's slutty, perturbed!
sweat poem? seldom published!"
sorry purveyor, sincerely.
P.S. stiff's perfume scent? perfect.

The River (of Fate)

By Almir Martin

To Me, From Years Ago

By Brianna Edgar

Life is a journey, one you so meticulously planned out.
But plans almost never go the way they should-
you already know that, don't you?
At seventeen you can't comprehend living any longer
gambling your life away
ready to end it all.

What if I told you
that your strife doesn't matter?
That in only a decade
you'll find yourself "fixing"
the mistakes you think you made?

There are no real mistakes in life
only choices directing you across different paths
shoving you into a reality
that would otherwise not exist.

I used to hate you.
I wanted you to have strength
something you hadn't experienced enough yet to possess.

Please forgive me
for the sins of my past,

because to you, they are still to come.

Mother Tree

By Elizabeth Holloway

The impregnable oak tree still allows
her supple and malleable arms to ebb and flow
with the pull of the wind. She will
still endure the foliage's tinkle at her toes,
the vast fields of dark green arugula and
other various fruitful vegetation.

Indubitably the insects inquire her
wisdom, resting graciously under the
chandelier of shade she produces.
Come rainfall she downs drops like
Daiquiris, obtaining all she needs
to continue her eloquent nature.

Birds take refuge within her fluttering,
butterfly-kiss embrace, basking in her maternal
emanance. All gather amiably with the bubbly
drunkenness of security, admiring the leaf ladies'
spectacle of graceful shimmer. A dance demanding
tranquility, luring the folk with their lullabies.

As dusk claims the sky, inflicting heavy eyes,
still, she cradles the critters in her battered
branches, within her webwork of netted arms.
Toasting their toes in her mantal of cherishment.

As elder rings wrinkle in her core, and the circle of life

claims the passing seasons, generations lay to rest
        in her wake. She offers a final kiss goodnight,
and a promise "Like you're mother and father before,
each intricate stroke of you're ancestry, I shall
carry you within your children, and theirs to come."

65

Poem Written During the Solar Eclipse

By Kane Driscoll

It looks like somebody took a big bite out of the sun
is how she described it to me.
We did what any reasonable person would do:
go to Dairy Queen, buy two chili cheese dogs, two blizzards,
go to an old, rusty, spraypainted train bridge
and watch the eclipse.

I went outside, a few minutes before it even started.
I wanted to see it begin.
I felt odd standing outside, looking up at the sun
(of course with proper eye protection—thanks Menards)
and went back inside, deciding it too early. I saw
the moon nibble the sun twenty minutes later though.
That's when we went to Dairy Queen.

I kept looking up during the drive
and could see the progress the moon made.
Faster than I expected,
although I knew the time everything would happen.

As it reached maybe 70% in the sky,
I noticed the humor:
all I could see of the sun,
the sliver of gold still glowing,
was nothing more than a crescent moon.

I knew it wouldn't get dark here,

sadly only reaching around 92% coverage,
but as the moon continued feasting
I noticed the edges of the world
where people forget to look,
and the sky was grey, muddled,
flat. As the moon continued
its path, it only crawled closer
from the edges, and it
looked like the colors of life
had almost become desaturated.
It jumped to dusk, not night,
gradiently, in a few minutes.

You

By Dominic Tatrai

You sit down to read this. The title caught your interest, if only sparingly, and the length isn't long (*three pages? Easy street.*) so if the story proves to be a waste of time, you will not have lost much. But the use of second-person catches you off-guard, as well as the narrator, who keeps translating your thoughts into black ink on white. You consider setting aside the story—which only continues to reveal itself as a weird distraction—but you soldier on, even if your patience is being stretched thin.

It's at this point in the narrative that you get up and grab a glass of juice. Yet you're confused; you didn't intend to get up, nor do you have juice (too much sugar). Yet you do it anyway. You down the sugary drink and when you're done, you lick your lips.

Once done with the lip-licking, you return back to the story, but the story isn't done with you yet. You hear scratching from the other room; you're the only one home, so you thought, but for some reason you're not startled. You get up and find the source of the sound; your pet rat, Dennis. You don't like rats, or rodents, or animals all that much. Even humans rub you the wrong way, most of the time. But you now have a Dennis-named rat to care for, locked up in a wire cage the size of an armoire. You don't know what an armoire is, but you imagine it to be big. You also have no clue how to take care of rats, let alone

rats named Dennis, and neither does the narrator: but
for this lone moment in time, Dennis, the whiskered
thing you've now been shackled with, looks at you with
a look that can only describe one thing: hunger. You
reach, without thinking, without even *wanting*, to the
bag of Doritos beside the cage-oire, and you hand the
rat a chip (you don't question if rats can even *eat* chips,
so don't even think about it). It eats greedily, and you
almost forget your complete revulsion for anything
rodent. Then you remember, and you shudder, and you
back away from the thing in the cage and return to the
story.

At this point you want to stop reading, yet the
words compel you to drive ahead. You now find yourself
as a frog; sickly green and slimy. You hate frogs more
than you hate rats; maybe your new amphibian nature
is a sign of a deep-seated self-loathing buried way down
in your heart? The narrator would like to remind you
to throw away such thoughts. You are a frog simply
because he wishes you to be. And now you're human
again. But five pounds heavier, as punishment for not
remembering who's in charge around here.

Your name is now Gennifer, and you're in the
retirement home. You've been waiting months for your
grandkids to visit. They don't even know what home
you're in. Now your name is Simmons, and you work
two weeks a month on an oil rig. They had to take
most of your right hand last winter. Frostbite's a killer.
Now you're the rat, Dennis, and you see your own
human hand dangling a Dorito over your head, but
it never drops. The human you wears a wicked smile.
You're not used to seeing your face look so cruel, your
hate so tangible. And now you're the narrator. You
type out inhumanities at your keyboard, but they're all
self-directed. You don't know why.

Finally, you're *you* again, reading this story. It appears to be drawing to a close. You're like a prisoner up for parole. You look at the field of beautiful white space up ahead, you ready yourself to greet it with open arms. But the narrator would like to remind you of the barbarism of the world. The narrator would like to remind you of hardship, disease, hurt, long hours wasted and sweet moments gone without warning. The narrator would like to remind you that everyone has a narrator, a warden that knows your pain, knows your pressure points, knows where to push to make you cry, make you shout, make you mean. Everyone has a narrator that makes the one in this story look like Mickey Mouse. At least here on the page, someone else is in control, someone incapable of truly breaking you down, turning you into the monster you hate to love.

So feel free to re-read this as many times as you need. Or enjoy the white space, and all it threatens.

ode to my melancholy
By Samantha Dave

after Olivia Gatwood's "Ode to my Jealousy"

you're the sweet eternal flame
ignited by a mother's kiss
& fueled by my shiny tears
fiery-red dragon protecting
the treasure in my mountain
chasing off visitors
& licking my wounds
pledging loyalty to only me
a stalled car stopping
oxygen from entering my lungs
choking down petroleum
until i retreat back to your home
bright orange traffic cones
and flashing red lights
tell me to proceed with caution
toward the only lit streetlight
at the end of my block
where a bat sleeps alone
you're the bottle of strawberry wine
waiting for me in my fridge
soaking up my sadness & storing
it for later, for the chance to pour
it over me like pig's blood
when i'm turning in my bed
like it was a game all along
like you wanted to see
how far i would run
because you know
i always come back

To crave union

By Draya Raby

After "Tether of Yearning" by Robert Fanning

I wait in heat, the writhing desert sun
His lips. His skin.
Our heartbeats become cairns.

That unique fun, that time just
before spring has sprung.
I wait like frog, crouched

Tongue stored curled
Inside my mouth, it waits
To jump, to flick.

Opisthosoma starved,
Web in creation and the spider
Licks her lips.

That distinct gray of storm,
That sprinkle before the pour,
That tingle in a deer's ear when

The smell of man wafts
Like the wind of ancestor spirits
I've prayed to hear.
I've prayed to feel your presence near.
I am fox as it waits on all fours,
Listening, for the signaling squeak of hunts jump.

In the time of drought my soil split,
Birthed a ravenous ravine ready to receive
The fruits of longed labor,

The sweet nectar beacon,
Aesculus pavia,
I crave our union.

a poet is the only god i'll worship

By Megan Monroe

life flows in rivers of ink and dusty
graphite, catching immortality in the space

between words. breath spills from periods,
heartbeats stilled in the curve of each comma

as golden ichor drips, searing the tongues
of mortals who try to mimic you. i thread

your touch through my veins, suture
my wounds with your marrow. the ink

on your fingers soaks my pulse; i bear
your gospel under my skin.

let me shape a mausoleum for your scripture
from tattooed bones and brittle paper.

anoint my hands with your fire;
i'll burn in worship, unashamed.

10 Questions

By Chandler Fox

A letter to ~~my brother~~ a soldier

By Eden Phillips

I keep imagining your face
at the other end of the gun.
Your eyes wide, the same as mine.
Would your hands shake?
Would you hesitate
if they told you I was the enemy?
I know you've never been a friend to me,
but a part of me became a part of you
in our mother's womb.
You have always preached family
when I strayed from God,
when I strayed from that trailer,
and the backwards roles we played
under one roof, one flag, one family.
A family that never liked me, but always loved me,
that could not agree or condone but they fed me.
And I think, in some ways you were right
that I could try to wash off the dirt
but this wrongness runs in our veins.
You will always carry our father's rage
as I carry our mother's lying tongue.
But I still covered your ears,
when their screams rattled the drywall.
So tell me now, as you don this uniform
and sign your soul away,
do you mean it now, that blood runs thicker
than water? These rising tides coming to drown me,

or will you believe them when they tell you
that your own brother is your enemy?
Will your hands shake?
Will you hesitate?
Are you more man or a soldier now?
What does your God say?

After Living Out of the Car for Three Days on Vacation

By Cailey Calhoun

walking across the Vegas strip   we were catcalled
I wasn't even wearing   a crop top

but maybe you were   we weren't even in sight of him for more
than four seconds   but maybe we were

we didn't look   we didn't say anything to each other
but maybe I should've   we just kept on north

we just kept searching for the   Bellagio fountains we
kept pretending   we didn't hear the whistle

the shout
      damn ladies that's some ass

we didn't want to say it was real   we wanted
to roll our eyes at this   silly story after dinner

we even had our hair up   we didn't have on makeup
all these words bounced between us   leashed to our sides

in the crowd   as the sun went down
if we said our thoughts out loud   everyone else would vanish

and we'd be right back crossing   staring that man down
and he would somehow still   win

so we didn't   we only pointed out the fake Eiffel tower
and told each other how much our feet   hurt

A Love Poem, Some Sort Of A Love Poem

By Elizabeth Holloway

Okay so here's what I've got:
Straight from the alarm to the Nespresso machine.
Velvety foam mustache bubbling in anticipation of
bitterness, cut with sweet chocolate cream. A warmth
washing away the morning sheath. Sweet cries of my
child, a single mother's morning symphony. Fill his
bowl with kibble, maybe a treat or two, absorb his
melodic purr in my fingertips. Lean into the meditative
realm behind my headphones. Perhaps a podcast
about Dostoevsky or the current political attack on
science. Drown my face in various lavish creams and
serums. By now the words are bubbling and boiling
over, spill some out onto a page or two in my journal.
What is every item I could possibly need for the day.
Packed. The interlude of the evening's tasks. Sticky
note to-do list, chronologically cross it in pen. Productive.
Fit in some weights, cardio, possibly a library session.
Home and into the shower. Scrub off the world with
those little vanilla scented rocks. Repeat creams and
serums. Lulled by the onset of the day's completion.
Book, gummy, movie, perhaps a video game or two.
Minty breath, crawl into bed. Before unconscious
takes over, bask in it. The beauty, the simplicity. Allow
its sweet nectar to fill your limbs. Slowly let it slosh
around, grow and fill. Until it reaches your toes, the
tip of your head. God, I can't wait to make my coffee
tomorrow.

life lessons defined by a two-year-old
By Megan Miller

1.) *i run:* a good way to exercise
   a good way to fall into a hardwood floor
2.) the best stuffed animals: one-eyed, patched holes,
 lumpy stuffing, dangling threads
3.) *if the light is green, mama goes, go mama, I'm hungry*
4.) *it's MINE:* anything not nailed to the floor
   anything handed to a sibling
5.) things that can be dipped in ranch: ~~anything~~ *not*
 oreos, icky
6.) if told "no" when asking for a snack, ask someone else
   *repeat until you get a "yes"
7.) there will be times where you count to twelve and
 fall back to seven
8.) you really can dance like nobody is watching
   *if it's to the beat of *baa baa yes sir*
9.) *what's its nom?*
  goats = *baas*
   sheep = *baas*
    cows = ~~moos~~ *cows*
10.) always have a clock around even if you can't read it
11.) the best perspective is achieved from a pair of glasses
   *glasses must be upside down, plastic, lime-
 green, absolutely NO lenses
12.) *i need a nap*
7.) there will be times where you count to twelve and
 fall back to seven
8.) band-aids: a synonym for stickers, both have dinosaurs

paper: a synonym for our bodies, dinosaurs can be
   stuck on them
9.) it's okay to tell someone you feel *yucky*
10.) morning: a doctor taking a cat's blood pressure, *a*
   shot in the butt fix him
   afternoon: a chef cooking an onion in a teacup, *i*
   make coffee
   evening: *i'm a witch   boo!*
11.) *ice is too hot to eat*
12.) adults appreciate a good hug
   especially the ones that *need a nap*

sexy

By Caitlin Berney

after Olivia Gatwood

i don't know if i will ever not be reminded that i am—
at least to you. even when my tears collect in puddles
on the divots in my collarbones, *sexy*
you say, as you sip them like white wine.
the way my laughter sways on the rim of a breaking glass,
shimmering, sharp, one breath away from shattering.
my hips an invitation mapped in curves,
sexy, like the sweetness of tangerines in summer sun,
the way it lingers, a symphony of thrill,
but why does my heart ache in the tune,
the echoes tinged with the salt of hesitation,
the question trailing me,
will there ever be a moment, a pulse,
when i don't feel the weight of your gaze,
like a coin heavy on my chest, *sexy*,
when i played at being invisible, yet glittered,
sexy, and still, in every murmur of night, i wonder if,
wrapped in comfortable darkness, i am just breath,
or if i am something more akin to a wildfire,
brimming with shame and flight, *sexy*,
an embodiment of desire in my own right,
or a whispered soul cast from clay,
the longing that floods from my heart,
sexy, the word that feels like a curse and a gift,
like honey dripped onto a blade—sweet, but slicing
and *sexy*, a moth mistaking the porchlight for the moon,
wings burning in its own devotion.

sexy, a necklace i never asked for,
clasped too tight, etching its name into my skin,
leaving an imprint even when it's gone,
a ghost of hands tracing places they do not own,
a shadow i cannot outrun.
is there a way to swallow my body back into itself,
to exist without being devoured?
sexy, a tide I never called,
but it pulls me under just the same,
like the moon dictating the rise and fall of my breath,
like saltwater licking the edges of a name written in sand,
erasing, returning, never truly gone.
sexy, i fill my exhale with the weight of wanting to be seen,
and inhale again with the willingness to hide.

Perfectionist

By Almir Martin

Like Father, Like Son

By Isabella Tucker

Based on the painting, Ivan the Terrible and His Son Ivan
on November 16, 1581, *Ilya Repin*

I.
You shouldn't be surprised,
yet the betrayal tastes as acrid
as the blood in your mouth. It drips
down the side of your face,
a mocking imitation of the tears
you cannot bring yourself to shed.

Every time he crossed the line
you moved the goalposts further
and further back, a new point of no return.
But now, the points of no return
have themselves reached a point
of no return. You've walked yourself
off the edge of a cliff
into the churning black waves below.

He cradles you like fine china
only now that you're slipping
through his fingers. His tears
drip onto your face and his hand
presses into the gaping wound
he gave you, the touch like fire
compared to his former frigidity.

Neither of you should be surprised,
yet you are. If you treat porcelain

like stone, eventually it will crack,
and the cracks will break,
and the breaks will crumble,
and crumble
          and crumble
                  and crumble
into a million tiny pieces.

Like father, like son.
An endless cycle of
terrible,
terrible,
terrible.

II.
It is only with the sickening crack
of the blow against his skull that you realize
you perhaps, maybe, just possibly
have gone a little bit too far. The noise laves
away your anger and swirls
it down the drain, leaving only a mild surprise.

You're crying and cradling him.
How many times had you shunned him
for the same weakness, for begging
at the altar of your feet for scraps
of love like a lowly mutt?
Stop crying over nothing. He was nothing
to you (wasn't he?) yet you weep regardless.

You press your hand to the gaping wound
you gave him and realize with startling clarity
you cannot put him back together.
You've been cracking, *breaking* him,
and throwing away each chipped off piece

for so long you wouldn't even know where
to start now that he has crumbled
into a million tiny pieces.

It is only with his dying breaths
as a rattling requiem that you realize
this is not how you were supposed
to love him. The black hole of rage
consumed everything else
you were supposed to feel.
Were you proud of him, once?
Are you proud of what you have turned him into?

The sins of the father
lies cold and dead.
Maybe it is you who is
terrible,
terrible,
terrible.

Echo and Narcissus

By Alyssa Moore

After Echo and Narcissus *by John William Waterhouse*

I.
Do you know how ridiculous you look right now?
Lazing next to the river like a dog in the sun
while I wait for your attention, *I am right here.*
I cannot fathom why I am doing this
you are *obsessed* with yourself.
So wrapped up in your complexion, the bridge of your nose,
your cupid bow, your cheekbones, the way your eyes
glisten in the water,
the way your hair falls
perfectly around your face
to frame your features,
it is outrageous but
I cannot help my jealousy of your eyes
why do they get to gaze upon you for so long?
Would living in your mind be the only way to love you?
And of course I wait for your eyes to flicker up to me.
I will wait inevitably for your eyes to meet mine
Even if for a moment
A moment of bliss.
For me of course, not you,
for you it will be like looking at a tree
or maybe, if I am lucky, a boar.
Maybe then I will see some kind of emotion from your face
other than infatuation with yourself.
I will wait
I will keep waiting
I will wait until I wither,

despite knowing you are never
going to look at me the way you look at you.

II.
Indulge me, take me in all of my glory.
My face, sculptors weep at the notion of never creating
such perfections.
These cannot be replicated by the hands of man.
How the sun kisses my skin
in a way no man or woman could,
the warmth wraps me like linen from a wash.
I pity the foolish scholars' attempts at describing my visage
for no one can put me onto paper.
Such a reflection should be forbidden.
For I am a sight to behold.
Aghast! Why do wrinkles suddenly fall upon my face
like rainfall?
You.
Bird!
Feathered and small with your beakish face
and shrieky song, stop
Stop fluttering your wings I cannot see
myself! These trees do not reflect me
the way the river's flow can, your meek
form takes up too much space, you must leave,
leave like the wind in the trees
to your slum
for you do not need the river
I *do*
a bird does not need to know what it looks like
for they all look the same,
your beauty is *simple* and *vague*, but me?
Me? I am the image of beauty
for what do buttercups and lilypads amount to
when I am beside them?

elegy for my mother

By Samantha Dave

for debbie wilder

I cling to old birthday cards and photographs
the way vodka clings to my mother's breath.
she tells me I'm wrong and that my memory is hazy,
like the morning fog that blinds my headlights
so that even they cannot see through the thickness
of lies about my childhood that I conjugate in my head.
my mother is present like a ghost—
her shadow roams the house without her
as she stays lost, a jane doe, with translucent skin
hiding blown-out veins in her arms and legs.
in times when I think she's poking through the mask
she tells me she loves me and that she's going to be better.
the next day she's gone, and my wallet is missing $50.
Mother, why did you hide in the bathroom
while my daughter fell out of the treehouse?
Once, we got in a fight, and she cut my hair
with a knife caked in chicken grease she pulled from the sink—
when I showed my father, he warned with a sigh
through a cloud of cigarette smoke
that I shouldn't bite the hand that needs me.

baptism

By Eden Phillips

I was washed new in the quarry
a quarter mile from the road
we stripped down to our skin
with the minnows, brushing against my calf
and you held me underwater
only long enough to make my heart skip
I broke the surface gasping,
my false prophet, my lucid dream
I left the water altered, I left the water clean

Clearwater Beach

By Cailey Calhoun

 I'll talk about the water,
swimming in it, like a memory
that feels like a dream.

There's water bigger than a bathtub
bigger than a pool or pond.
The ocean reaching for the
horizon, kissing the clouds.

Above the surface sits creamy
white beachside and to my right
my sister splashes in high tide.

And below the waves are the folds
between book pages and the atoms
of air between plant roots. The water
as infinite as those spaces unseen.

On the cusp of the two I am floating
on my back, arms out and feet flexed up,
like a crucifix-shaped baptism.

I am looking up into the sun-painted
streaks of pink, watching specks
of birds, completely weightless
in the hold of the salt and sea.

My ears are covered, sound slipping
in and out. I'm bobbing right between.
Shushing waves hold me gently

like they're holding this world in their
left hand and the next in their right,
while letting me stretch out between
the two as a buoyed offering.

bitter fruit

By Caitlin Berney

their hand rests on my hip,
light as a seed husk—
feels like the weight
of overripe fruit splitting open.
juice runs beneath my skin,
thick and sticky,
rotting sweet.
breath like warm honey—
it coats my throat,
too rich, too thick.
my stomach twists,
sour pulp rising up.
fingers skim my ribs
like peeling back citrus rind,
the tender white beneath
already bruising.
the acid burns.
their mouth tastes like wine,
fermented and sharp.
teeth brush my lip—
a bite—
the taste of iron blooms
like biting into a pomegranate seed,
dark and metallic.
i swallow too hard,
the pit lodging in my throat.
their hands press deeper—

kneading soft dough—
but my skin resists,
stretching too thin.
it's too much.
sugar-crusted fear,
the ache of something raw
beneath the sweetness.
i pull away,
the taste of bitter fruit
still curling on my tongue.
i feel their gaze,
ripe with patience,
but my skin has already
closed in on itself,
peach flesh stiffening
beneath the bruise.
a hand lingers at my wrist—
gentle pressure—
but my body has hollowed out,
the pit left behind.
i shake my head,
acid curling at the back of my throat.
the sweetness is gone now,
just the sharp tang of rind,
the bitter skin
of something once whole.

Meet the Contributors

Shy Barteck is a Michigan based artist whose mediums of preference include photography, writing, and sculpture. Located in the middle of the mitten surrounded by freshwater lakes, she was raised in the light of campfires and fireflies. She is a non-traditional, first-generation college student. Shy currently attends Central Michigan University as a full-time student, on course to graduate this May with a BFA in Studio Art with an emphasis in Photography. She received an Associate in Applied Science Degree, Graphic Design with Honors in May 2023 from Mid Michigan College. Shy is also a mother of three daughters, wife of almost a decade, business owner, plus an undeniable coffee, cat, and chicken lover.

Aphelion Bates is a nonbinary fourth year student living in Midland, Michigan. They are studying Secondary Math Education at CMU while taking the Creative Writing Certificate on the side. While they hope to be a high school math teacher in the future, they take great joy in writing poetry and fiction in their spare time, with a focus on trans and queer topics.

Caitlin Berney is an English Education and Creative Writing senior at Central Michigan University. A variety of her work has been published in previous editions of *Central Review*. Caitlin hopes to become an English and Creative Writing teacher and will be starting her student teaching in the fall of 2025. She can't wait to begin inspiring students to find life though language!

Kaelynn Blake is a poet from Grandville, Michigan. Her work has previously appeared in *The Central Review* last spring, and largely focus on nature and her own experiences in the world. She is currently studying English Education at CMU with a minor in Creative Writing.

Cailey Calhoun is a junior at Central. She has been published twice previously in *Central Review*. She is studying Secondary English Education with hopes of becoming a middle or high school English teacher after graduation. She hopes to inspire her future students to become writers in her future classroom.

Samantha Dave is a third year English and psychology student from Lake Orion, Michigan. When she's not writing poetry, she can be found listening to music, reading a new book, or playing video games. Her favorite poets (though they are always changing) are currently Olivia Gatwood and W.H. Auden. She finds inspiration from the music she listens to, the relationships in her life, and the world around her. After graduating, she hopes to get her MFA in creative writing.

Kane Driscoll is a Master's student studying Creative Writing at Central Michigan University. His work has appeared in a variety of journals, including *Inscape*, *Central Review*, and *Eastern Iowa Review*. His work is often conversational and occasionally leans towards the absurd. When he is not writing, he can often be found staring out his window, reading, or playing video games.

Brianna Edgar is an English student living in Mount Pleasant. When she isn't writing, she can be found reading or playing video games. She loves her cat and finding new places to hide out with a silly little drink and a book.

Chandler Fox is an English Education major with a passion for art in all its forms. Collaborating with his best friend and muse, Lillian Scarborough, Chandler and Lily seek to push the boundaries of photography, creating thought-provoking images that invite reflection and challenge perception.

Aldo García-Pájaro hails from Port Huron, Michigan. His previous work has made award-winning appearances in *Patterns*, a literary and visual arts magazine published by St. Clair County Community College. He is devoted to psychology and French as a Multicultural Advancement Scholar and a member of CMU's Honors Program. He plans on studying abroad in France as an undergraduate student before pursuing a master's degree in industrial-organizational psychology.

Brittany Hanner is a writer currently residing in Mt Pleasant, Michigan. Her work has been featured in *Images Literary Magazine* and *The Central Review*. She is currently pursuing an English degree at Central Michigan University with a Creative Writing Certificate and hopes to pursue an MFA for Creative Writing.

Courtney Hanses is a writer from Westphalia, Michigan but stays in Mt Pleasant for the school year. She engages in many different mediums of creativity, including illustration, graphic design, photography, and fiction writing. She is working towards earning her BFA in Graphic Design. She hopes to publish more of her writing someday.

Elizabeth Holloway is a young writer born and raised in the Upper Peninsula of Michigan. She is currently residing in Mount Pleasant, studying English and Creative Writing at Central Michigan University. She hopes to further her education in writing and literature and pursue a career in which she can exercise those skills.

Morgan Hughley is a poetry writer from Detroit, Michigan. She always writes but has never shared her work. She hopes this submission marks the beginning of sharing more of her poetry. Currently, she is pursuing a degree in Integrative Public Relations at Central Michigan University and graduates in the spring!

Ella Hunnewell is a student at Central Michigan University. She is currently majoring in Psychology and minoring in Creative Writing, Spanish, and Women's and Gender Studies. She hopes to continue her education to become a clinical psychologist.

Aparnaa Iyer is currently pursuing a Master's in Economics degree here at CMU. Aparnaa loves reading books and self-published a small poetry book in May 2023, only in India, with the help of *Notion Press Publications*. Aparnaa is currently working on writing a romance novel, and plans to pursue a PhD in Economics and keep writing at the same time!

Gwendolyn Kilpatrick is an aspiring poet living in Troy, Michigan, and studying at CMU. She is a sophomore studying electrical engineering with a minor in math. She intends to continue with poetry as an extracurricular activity in conjunction with her studies and enjoys the work of Sylvia Plath, Giacomo Leopardi, and Mary Oliver.

Autumn Malinowski is currently a junior at Central Michigan University. She is in the dual degree program pursuing a B.A.A. in Commercial Music and a B.A. in English, while getting a Creative Writing certificate. In the future, she hopes to work in the music industry as a songwriter or a live sound engineer.

Almir Martin is an artist/designer from Gary, Indiana. He's currently studying graphic design and cultural competency at Central Michigan University. Over the past year he worked with Israel Davis to bring artist Thomas Lucas to give demos and a lecture on campus, even designing the posters. Blending a myriad of influences, styles, and aesthetics, he aims to give others a glimpse into the world in his mind, whatever that looks like.

June Maslowski is a strange gal from the midwest. Poetry is her way of making a puzzle because she was always awful at puzzles. Enjoy.

Megan Miller is a junior from Bad Axe, Michigan. Her work has previously appeared in *Central Review*. She is currently majoring in English and minoring in Public Law, Creative Writing, and History at Central Michigan University. Outside of writing, Megan enjoys crocheting, trivia, reading, and attending the theatre with her family and friends.

Carter Moleski is a math education major pursuing a certificate in Creative Writing at Central Michigan University. His writing explores the intersections of music and nature, drawing inspiration from artists such as Jaimie Branch, Archy Marshall, and Kara Jackson.

Megan Monroe is a senior at Central Michigan University, earning a BA in English Literature with a focus in Creative Writing. She is also enrolled in CMU's Accelerated MA program for Creative Writing. A variety of her work has appeared in *The Central Review*.

Alyssa Moore is an artist and student living in Grand Blanc, Michigan. She's currently a student at Central Michigan University majoring in Studio Art and is currently working on a Creative Writing certificate. Her best work comes to her while she's in the middle of something else. Always.

Tarry Palmer is a non-traditional student at Central Michigan University. He is working on his bachelor's degree in history and is enrolled in the Accelerated Masters program in English—Creative Writing. His goal is to work in historical research and write books, both fiction and poetry, on the side.

Eden Phillips is a poet from Stockbridge, Michigan. He is currently studying English at Central Michigan University with minors in Creative Writing and Intergroup Relations and Justice, and is the president of Wordhammer, the performative poetry club on campus.

Draya Raby is a journalism and creative writing student at CMU. Through her time in the Creative Writing program, she has developed a deep love for poetry as a form of emotional expression. Her creative work has not yet been published but through an internship with WCMU Public Media, she has had numerous journalism stories published. Being a writer has always been her dream, and the Creative Writing program has helped make that dream feel possible.

Lillian Scarborough is a junior at Central Michigan University. She is currently pursuing a Secondary English Ed Major with a Creative Writing minor. She enjoys studying creative writing personally, but she believes it will equip her with the skills to create an engaging and inclusive environment for her future classrooms.

Rowan Schachermeyer is a writer from Chesterfield, Michigan. He is currently studying Creative Writing and Psychology at Central Michigan University, and hopes to pursue a Master's in Creative Writing as well.

Madison Schamber is a sophmore from Fremont, Michigan currently majoring in English with a minor in Creative Writing. This is her second year publishing with *Central Review*. She's a passionate writer and she hopes to pursue her writing career in the Accelerated Master's program at CMU in the future, and go on to write professionally.

Janessa Shepard is a graduate student in Creative Writing. Her work has appeared in *The Honors Platform* and *Central Review* journals. She grew up on a farm in a small West Michigan town and is close to nature and her family.

Masha Smahliuk is a junior at Central Michigan University, majoring in Journalism and minoring in Creative Writing. She is a managing editor at Central Michigan Life. But she also loves writing fantasy books and poetry.

Gabrielle Steele, otherwise known as Gabbi, is a current second year student at Central Michigan University. She is currently studying Secondary English Education with a certificate in Creative Writing, and she hopes to make the world a better place through her teaching and her writing.

Hannah Stout is a graduate student at CMU who will be graduating this May with her Master's in Creative Writing. She is sad to leave Mt. Pleasant, but is happy to have made the friends and memories in her four short years here. If Hannah had one wish it would be to grow taller.

Dominic Tatrai is a student living in Mt. Pleasant, Michigan. He is currently studying Creative Writing at Central Michigan University, where he hopes to complete a master's degree in the same field. He has two gerbils and a hamster, who may be the true authors of this piece.

Kayla Thatcher currently resides in Mt. Pleasant, Michigan, where she is studying Sociology and earning a Creative Writing minor at Central Michigan University. Some of her work can be found in *Central Review*.

Isabella Tucker is a Central Michigan student who grew up in Ann Arbor, Michigan. They enjoy creative writing in their free time, especially poetry, as well as creating visual art. They are currently majoring in secondary education (mathematics).

Meet the Staff

Liv O'Toole is a fourth-year English student and first-year Creative Writing master's student from Saginaw, Michigan. Her hobbies include listening to Taylor Swift and just kinda wandering around. Liv's favorite genre of anything is fantasy, and in her spare time, she plays video games like Skyrim, Dragon Age, and The Witcher 3. Her favorite poets are Pablo Neruda and Mary Oliver. This is her second year as an Editor-in-Chief of *The Central Review*.

Brenna Dean is a first-year Creative Writing master's student. She loves sitting in the sun with her kitten, watching movies with friends, visiting her dogs, and doing all sorts of crafts. She's always looking for another concert to attend with her best friends, another opportunity to write poems on Beaver Island, and another recipe she'll probably never bake. After graduation, she hopes to pursue her MFA and spend more time staring up at the stars. This is her first year as Editor-in-Chief of *The Central Review*.

Bri Edgar is an English student from Hartland, MI. When she isn't working or in class, she is constantly on her computer working on whatever she's writing at the time. She loves fantasy romance novels, playing on her switch, and pro wrestling.

Lauren Cole is a fourth year Secondary Education major from Saginaw! She likes video games like Overwatch and Skyrim, reading, and hanging out with her friends while watching an F1 race. After graduation, she wants to teach History and Mythology, and have at least four cats!

Madison Schamber is a second-year English and Creative Writing student from Fremont, Michigan. She loves playing casual, cozy video games such as the Sims 4 and also playing DND. She is also obsessed with cats and currently has 7 in total. One fun fact about her is that she is currently learning Japanese and hopes to study abroad in Japan soon. After graduation, she plans to write her own fantasy and romance novels and become a published author.

Corey Hogue is a third-year English Major/Journalism Minor and a creative writer from Detroit, Michigan. Aside from reading/writing, Corey also is interested in journalism, drawing, and similar mediums in his life's quest to "tell a story." He enjoys playing 4x and role-playing games such as Songs of Syx and exploring and researching the mythology of various peoples like the ancient Irish and Anglo-Saxons.

Samantha Dave is a third-year English and Psychology student from Lake Orion, Michigan. When she is not writing poetry, she can be found listening to music, reading a new book, or playing video games. Her favorite poets are Karyna McGlynn and W. H. Auden. After graduating, she hopes to work with a publishing company reading manuscripts! This is her first year working with *Central Review*.

Cailey Calhoun is a Junior here at Central. She is studying Secondary English Education while also pursuing a minor in Creative Writing. She is the Treasurer of Sigma Tau Delta at Central. She is from a tiny town east of Grand Rapids called Lowell, Michigan. In her free time, Cailey likes to read as much as she can, write tons and tons of mediocre poetry, and go on very long walks through campus and the parks around town. She is a book nerd through and through who hopes to instill a love of literature in her future students as a teacher.

Em Hazel is a bright-eyed elusive manic currently holding the role of a Junior at Central Michigan University. She has always dedicated herself to majoring in English, not to mention the Creative Writing minor, but has also taken up a Logistics Management and Marketing major to complement the controlling slytherin-istic aspects inside of her. To walk the fine line of art and business involves a special curation of growing up in the same house, in the quaint town of Swartz Creek, and traveling with her family to the far reaches of land and sea. When not sitting by a window with a steaming cup of herbal tea, book in hand, she is sitting somewhere in the sun writing down every thought that needs ink and paper to listen. Only during her free time does she get scheduled to work as the shift lead at her job (for now). She has two black cats and her favorite number has always been 13, yet she has a steady boyfriend of seven years and her biggest dream is to open a florist shop to sell some of the fresh flowers she and he will grow together.